Be Confident! You are Special

A kid's book about believing in yourself and
developing self-esteem

MARTINA GROEN

To my children, George and Richard, may they always be free to be themselves. Let them follow the guiding star that will show them the way, their way, that will make them feel like they are home.

CONTENTS

INTRODUCTION

I decided to write these stories imagining that the characters in them might resemble you, speak to you, represent you, and whose story might be yours.

Identifying with someone else's life is a beautiful exercise for sharing emotions, a way to know each other deeply, and to discover ourselves. It's like standing in front of a mirror; our image is reflected without any filters, without masks, without extravagance.

They are wonderfully free to be themselves.

And just as an archer shoots his arrow, I release mine, which goes straight into your hearts. For every one of you, I would like to erase the inadequacy, fear, discouragement, and other feelings that snuff out your internal light.

I hope I'll make you experience moments of lightheartedness, joy, and tenderness.

The perfect storm doesn't exist; the moment when everything is unique and ready doesn't exist. Overthinking about things doesn't always lead to the right answer.

You only need to be brave, have faith in yourself, and trust in the voice inside, in our hearts, that tells us to *live, experience, try and get involved.*

So, between doing and not doing, **always choose doing**. If you try yet do something wrong, it doesn't mean you're failing because you've already placed a pebble on your path. You've already marked the way that will lead you to the goal. **And don't be afraid to start over. At any time.**

Be true to yourself, don't judge yourself, respect yourself, love yourself and reward yourself because you're you and no one is like you.

We're all different, all extraordinarily perfect, just as we are.

This book will make you travel to different places while sitting in your armchair. You'll cross Tunisia, Sweden, Holland, Italy, France, America, and finally, Albany. Every story keeps the real essence of each country; you'll sense different tastes and smells of that land. The characters are real, common people; you'll be able to relate to them and mix with their lives.

All the stories follow a thread that connects them: **morals**.

Never lose heart! We only need to close our eyes, listen to our hearts, and follow our path. Every one of us has our own distance to cover, but with courage and dedication, we can all get to the same door, the door of **fulfillment**.

The stories' pictures are intentionally black and white to leave room for your imagination. Choose your own colors and try to color every picture based on the emotions you felt as you read or listened to each story. This will become a perfect exercise to turn this book into your unique and special book.

Now turn this page; the stories' train is about to leave.

Happy reading and, most importantly, bon voyage!

Djerba was his city. He was born there, breathing the saline air of his sea, the Mediterranean Sea. Hot and salty during the summer, cold and stinging during the winter. A fascinating pearl of the Mediterranean, whose sky is always blue, the legend says that the particular climate of Djerba urged Ulysses' companions to stay on the island forever.

He was proud of his land. When he was little, he told everyone he was born under a very tall palm tree, drinking milk and eating delicious dates and sweets. Samir was his name, an important name. Even his grandpa's name was Samir, a tall man who was a bit crabby with everyone. But with Samir, his heart opened up, and he softened merely by looking at him.

Little Samir grew up well, jumping up and down in the large square near his house and helping his grandpa at his workshop. He was really good, talented, and creative, and in his hands, the wood took shape and form. He moved easily around his grandpa's workshop, an expert carpenter, and he knew every single tool and all their smallest secrets. His moves were like dancing, music, joy, and magic. Yes, magic! Who can start with a meaningless piece of wood, crooked and knotty, and end up with a chair, table, or bookcase? Only a magician can!

"Grandpa, see this piece of wood? I would like to turn it into an elegant desk."

"Samir, work hard, and I'm sure you'll get an awesome result."

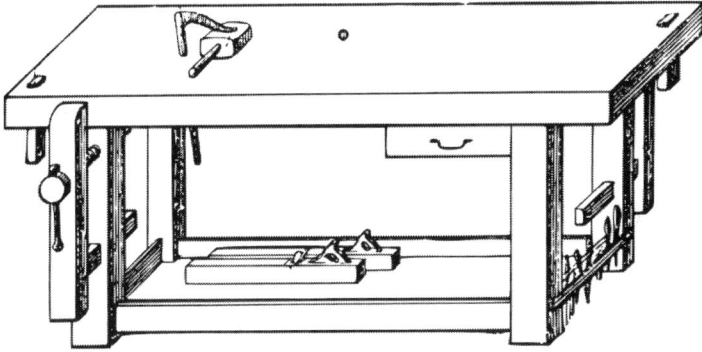

His grandpa was very proud of Samir, and even though he had some aches and pains because of his age, he worked without stopping. He was always there, in his small workshop lit up only by a small and dim light, next to Samir. He looked at him during his transformations, and under his long white mustache, there was always a bright smile.

One cold winter night, grandpa heard a small *click*. Right there, next to his heart.

He didn't want to make Samir worry, so he said: "*Samir, Grandpa is tired; let's close the workshop a bit early this evening, and let's go to sleep.*"

Samir looked at his dear grandpa, and in his small heart, he knew that something was wrong.

So, he said: "*Grandpa, I'll go home with you. It's cold outside, and you can rest on my shoulder; we'll get home faster that way.*"

His grandpa didn't hesitate. Under the cold light of a lamppost, Grandpa and Samir slowly crossed the long and silent square.

Samir opened the door to his home; he could still smell his Grandma Aida's perfume, who had flown to heaven a few months ago. Samir helped his grandpa change his clothes, and, finally, he too put his head on the pillow.

His grandpa, at that moment, took his grandson's hand and said: *"Go home now, it's night already, and I'm sure your mom is worried. I'm fine."*

Samir felt uneasy, but he knew his grandpa was right; his mom would definitely be worried about him.

But before leaving, the boy asked his grandpa: *"Grandpa, can you promise me something?"*

"Sure, tell me what it is," the grandpa answered.

"You'll always be next to me, right?"

His grandpa teared up; he knew he couldn't keep that promise as he was very old and sickly now. But he answered without hesitation: *"I'll always watch over you; my heart is yours, and my hands are your hands."*

Samir closed the door without looking him in the eye; he was deeply hit by those words. He ran, ran, and ran so fast his legs felt like burning missiles. He could only hear the sound of his shoes on the concrete.

When he got home, he heard his mom's voice calling him: *"Samir, where have you been? It's so late! You know that when it gets dark, I start worrying if I don't see you."*

Samir answered: *"Mom, I was at the workshop. Grandpa promised me something!"*

"And what did he promise?"

"Mom, promises are like secrets; you can't tell them to other people immediately."

Samir went straight to the kitchen. It was the warmest room of the house; the fire in the hearth crackled. He drank a cup of hot milk and ate a piece of his mom's donut; then, he immediately went to bed in his room that was lit only by the moon.

Early in the morning, Samir ran to the kitchen; the bread was fresh out of the oven, warm and fragrant.

"What a good smell, Mom! I'll take a piece for Grandpa too - what a delight it will be with your marmalade!"

Mom smiled at Samir; she enjoyed his compliments as they were delicate and loving, and then she said: *"I'll wait for you here, Samir. Don't be late, and give Grandpa a kiss when you see him."*

Samir left in a rush, jumping up and down the square. He got to the workshop all out of breath. The lights were off, and the door was still closed. How strange, he thought to himself. At a certain point, Samir's heart started beating fast and, like a rocket, he ran to Grandpa's home...

Ten long years went by, and Samir became a strong and even more talented boy. He was always there, at his grandpa's workshop, lit only by a dim light. He didn't want to change anything since the last time his grandpa worked there.

One morning, Samir was in the workshop, working at full speed. All of a sudden, the door opened up, and an elegant and refined man came in. He noticed the display, and he was fascinated with it.

"You'll be the one to furnish my home," he said decisively to Samir.

The boy enthusiastically accepted, but he was quickly taken over by despair: the delivery time was very tight, and, on his own, working all those pieces of wood was truly going to be a challenge.

Samir was sitting on an old stool. His dear grandpa always sat there. The workshop was always and only lit up by a small, dim light, but suddenly, the room became bright like a sunny day. Samir started jumping around the room as he did when he was a child and, at some point, he heard something.

He said: *"Grandpa, is that you? Do some magic, stay with me. Your heart is mine; your hands are my hands, remember?"*

Samir felt a strength inside himself he hadn't ever felt before and got started on his work immediately.

Long, sleepless nights went by in his grandpa's workshop and, just when the delivery day came, Samir screamed happily: *"Grandpa! Grandpa! I did it! I finished it all! Everything is ready!"*

He turned the doorknob of the workshop with all his strength, and then he ran, jumping up and down the square. He arrived at the gate of the enormous building, delivering all the requested materials. The pieces were truly unique, made of bright and shiny wood, polished one by one.

In the city, the news about Samir's talent spread like wildfire all the way to the capital, Tunis, and Samir became the most famous and requested carpenter in all of Tunisia.

To this day, Samir is still there, in his grandpa's small workshop, lit only by a small, dim light, sitting on the stool polishing and transforming pieces of wood.

His grandpa is still there keeping his promise, looking over him, his heart in his heart, his hands in his.

What does this story teach us?

Every one of us is born with a talent. It's a small, hidden gift that is given to us at birth. It's a special key that opens only one door; each has its own lock!

Sometimes the search for our talent is a real treasure hunt.

It's not always easy to find; sometimes, we're better at seeing it in others, recognizing great qualities, abilities, and capacities in others, and forgetting that we have them too.

In this story, we can see Samir's strength - the determination that leads him to take charge of his talent and make it magic.

So, if you have a dream, believe in yourself and listen to that voice deep inside your heart that points to the right way.

THE CHIMNEY SWEEP - STOCKHOLM, SWEDEN

In the labyrinth of cobbled streets in the cold city of Stockholm, a strange man had been wandering around for a few days: he was a chimney sweep.

He was a funny old man, a little clumsy and with a big belly. His hair was always messy and framed his face, his two cheeks as red as ripe pomegranates. He wore a strange black tracksuit, and he wore boots that were two sizes too big for him.

He walked up and down the streets of the city center with long and labored steps. In his hands, he carried a large brush, and while he was walking, he made long and loud moans. When people saw him, they were speechless; he was quite the character!

He always had breakfast at the same time, in the same bar, in his usual seat. A strong coffee and a honey-glazed donut, a glance at his favorite newspaper, and then he would go back to walking up and down again.

He always had a dark expression on his face, not because he was dirty, but because he was permanently filled with rage.

One day, while he was walking through the city center's streets with his usual long brush, a child sitting next to a fountain noticed him and started watching him with interest. The old man walked all over the place, muttering and grumbling. It seemed like he was angry with the whole world.

So, the boy approached him and asked: *"Why do you moan and complain all the time?"*

The old man stood silent for a moment; he wasn't expecting that intrusion. He wasn't used to dealing with other people, so, after a moment of hesitation, he answered: *"Ah, what do you want to know about my life? You're so young, my boy; if I were to tell you everything, a whole lifetime wouldn't be enough. I'm so black inside, not even just black; I'm filled with rage! The good times have passed; man has set foot on the moon, he discovered there's life on Mars, he went beyond the limits of medicine, and he invented molecular gastronomy. What does an old man like me count for, with his brush in his hand? Maybe I should just give up. I'm no use to anyone, and it's useless to think about* changing things, particularly dwelling on going back to the past."

While the old man was talking, the child looked at him carefully. He really was a very interesting guy. He sat down comfortably on the bench, more and more intrigued about his speech, and he asked: "*But what change are you waiting for?*"

The old man, tired of waiting for a miracle, sat down next to the child. He put the brush on the bench and said: "*You're such a dear, my boy. You have the same curiosity I had when I was young like you. There's a lot to tell, and my story is quite good. Do you want to listen to it?*"

The child smiled at him and said: "*Before we start, sir, I would like to introduce myself. My name is Ludvik; what about yours?*"

The old man started laughing; his mouth opened so much it looked like the mouth of a crocodile, and he said: "*My name is Ludvik too, and it fits me perfectly. It means glorious warrior. What a coincidence! But now, let's get to the story...*"

25

"I come from a line of famous chimney sweeps. My great-grandfather was one, my grandfather was one, and my father was also one. In my day, when you inherited a job, it was a true fortune. We used to work hard and a lot. I only thing in the house that could give some warmth was the fireplace; everyone had one. It had many uses, and it could work as a mixture of appliances put together. With the fireplace, you could warm up your house; you could cook with a pot on it; you could dry clothes there, and, at night, everyone gathered around the fire to create a wonderful atmosphere. There were so many nights next to the fire, but the one that is etched onto my heart was the one when my wife, in front of a dim light and crackling wood, told me I would become a father soon! How exciting!

"I was always on the go; when chimneys became clogged, they all called me to clean them. I knew all the chimneys in the city of Stockholm. I came back home covered from top to bottom in dirty soot; I was a black cloud. But I was happy because I

thought that, thanks to my work, a lot of families could warm themselves with the pleasant warmth of their chimney.

"Today, everything's changed, and innovation has given way to designer technological radiators that are almost invisible.

People are in a hurry, and they don't have time to snuggle in front of the fire anymore. This is why I'm angry; I don't have a job anymore, and maybe it's time I accept my retirement."

The chimney sweep's eyes were sad and melancholy. His story deeply touched the boy who was truly moved by it. They remained silent for a while, watching and scrutinizing each other. They had to find a solution as soon as possible.

Suddenly, the boy stood up from the bench. He hugged the old man and screamed: *"I've got it! What a brilliant idea! You have to meet my dad. He will help us, I'm sure."*

The boy's father was the director of a big shopping center, very famous in the city, and among the many different home items, there wasn't yet a space dedicated to fireplaces.

He waved goodbye to the old man in a great rush, with the promise to see him again. Right there, in front of the fountain, at the same time, the next morning. With a handshake, he sealed the promise, and he ran home.

Ludvik anxiously waited for the return of his father. When he got back, he barely had time to put his jacket and his hat on the coat rack before he heard:

"Dad! I have to tell you a story. Sit down, make yourself comfortable, listen, and then tell me what you think."

Ludvik's father did just that. He was a little surprised.

After his story, his dad was really touched by the old man's tale. He almost cried. He accepted his son's proposal with so much enthusiasm and joy that he immediately opened a new section in the shopping center dedicated exclusively to fireplaces, just like there used to be.

The boy hugged his dad, and he went straight to bed, but he couldn't fall asleep because he was so happy.

The next morning, while eating a cookie, he ran to meet up with the old man. And he was there; he had kept his promise!

Ludvik took him to his father's offices in the big shopping center, and they quickly became friends. His father suggested he tell his story to encourage young couples to buy a fire instead of a cold radiator.

It was an incredible success! All the people who were there for the opening of the new section were excited and moved by the fascinating story of the old man. Very soon, orders started to come in copious amounts: hundreds, perhaps even thousands of fireplaces.

The old man was finally happy because he could go back to his job and get his hands covered in soot again. He held the boy tightly to his chest, and with his other arm, he hugged his father.

This is how Stockholm, from above, came again to be a cloud of crackling chimneys.

Discovering our own talent and following the path it carves out for us doesn't have an end or a deadline. Our talent will stay with us forever.

The story of the chimney sweep suggests just so. The funny old man continues to have a job, the one he's always known how to do since he was a child.

His talent is so authentic that he's recognized even though time passes and even though there's innovation. This is exactly his strength: to make his talent shine and keep it current, matching the pace of change.

THE SECRET GARDEN - AMSTERDAM, HOLLAND

"*One, two, three, four, and five! Mom, mom, it's only five steps from the garden!*"

"*Isabel, you know the rules. I don't get how you can be bored; you have so much space and so many toys to choose from!*" her mom answered with a stern tone.

When I was a child, I counted the steps that separated me and a secret garden, closed off by a fence. Just like loyal soldiers, there were ancient oak trees and a very tall sequoia tree. I sat under that giant, and there, in the silence, I could feel the sky breathing.

We had just moved to this wonderful mansion, a little outside town, away from my Amsterdam. It was a unique city with its own style: its channeled waters follow you everywhere. The chimes of bike bells ring in your ears, culture and beauty fill your eyes, and you have the feeling of being surrounded by something that completes you.

My dad always ran away from the city. He loved the countryside, and he loved taking shelter between the colorful fields of tulips. On his bike, one day, he noticed a mansion. It was quite old and needed some sorting out, but he was so taken by it that when he saw it, he told mom he had the same feeling he had a lot of years prior when he hopelessly fell in love with her.

"I've been struck by so much beauty!" he pointed out.

Mom didn't really agree with him as she didn't like moving house. She was a woman who liked her routine, but she was completely overwhelmed by my father's energy.

They immediately started building works in the mansion, and many months passed before we could move in. The wait paid off, though. The house came alive and breathed again.

In a few weeks, we managed to move, and as promised by dad, before spring began, we were living there.

The home space was limitless, you could lose yourself in there, and mom was very good at furnishing the house. All the bedrooms were beautiful, they had a very old parquet floor, but mine was special.

I chose it immediately. It was big, bright, and it had a small fireplace. Under a big and colorful stained-glass window was a tall step with a big red velvet pillow on it.

The stained-glass window overlooked a gigantic garden that was neglected and surrounded by very tall trees. The garden belonged to the mansion, but it gave the impression it had been forgotten and abandoned.

The former owner made my dad promise that he wouldn't tidy up the garden. It had to stay that way – just as he had left it.

The secret garden impressed all the people that came to visit. Mom and Dad always changed the subject when they were asked why it was so neglected.

I wanted to know more too, but we had complete secrecy, so there was nothing to discuss.

During an afternoon at the beginning of spring, I was playing near the fence of the mysterious garden with my favorite doll, Camilla. At some point, there was a big gust of wind, strong and intimidating, and it blew open the small gate of the fence.

I immediately placed the bike under the sequoia tree, put my doll under my arm, and moved closer to the small gate.

It was all rusty, but the wind had managed to open it! I had to take advantage of the situation right away, but with caution. I had to make sure I wasn't seen by anyone, or I would have been in trouble.

I looked around carefully. There was no one in sight, so I went in walking on tiptoes.

I immediately had the feeling of being in a magical, timeless place.

The complete neglect had spoiled the garden, but you could tell it had originally been tended to with attentive care, love, and passion from the old owner. Everything smelled of beauty.

There were more than fifty bushes of roses of many different colors and shades: red, pink, white, yellow, then tulips, cyclamens, violets, and fields of daisies and sunflowers. There were rows of pine trees and cypresses, plus fruit trees: cherry trees, peach trees, lemon trees. At the center of the garden was a big fountain with five tanks, although it was turned off and there wasn't even a drop of water.

What a delightful smell you could inhale there.

So, I opened my arms, and I took a deep breath of that crisp air.

But, suddenly, a gust of truly mischievous wind moved a huge chain.

Attached to the branch of an enormous tree, there was a swing that was still in perfect condition. I sat on it immediately, and I started swinging backward and forward. I went so high it seemed like I touched the sky. How can a garden so big and beautiful be abandoned, I asked myself?

I had been playing there for a while, so, moved by an uncontrollable sense of guilt, I left. I delicately closed the small gate, leaving a small space open, and I went running home like a gazelle.

Mom saw me running at the entrance and stopped me.

"Hey! What's with all the panting? Where have you been? I've been looking for you for a while. You're all sweaty," she said to me.

My face was red, my cheeks rosy, like ripe apples; they were burning, my dress full of weeds. Sweat-dripping curls poked messily out of my blonde braid. My heart was beating fast, I wasn't used to lying to my mom, but I had to. She would forbid me from going to the secret garden again if I told her everything.

So, without looking at her in the eyes, I said: "Mom, don't you see it's spring? There's life outside of here!"

My mom smiled, and while I was going to the bathroom, I saw out of the corner of my eye that she hadn't stopped looking at me.

I immediately had a hot bath, full of bubbles, and while I was there, pampered by the soft suds, I promised myself I would go to the old owner to find out the mysterious secret about the garden.

Every afternoon, at the same time, when the air was fresher, I went out to the courtyard, placed my bike under the sequoia tree, and I went inside the garden. I felt free and calm. There was still life in there! I hadn't to waste any more time; everything that was there had to be taken care of and watched over.

I armed myself with courage, closed the small gate, and went towards the old owner's house on my bike.

I rang the bell, and she opened the door. She had in her arms a beautiful cat with black and shiny fur.

She looked at me, gave me a warm smile, and said: *"Hello dear, what brings you here?"*

Those words resonated with me like music.

"The wind of curiosity," I answered cheerfully.

We immediately started laughing together. Her name was Annette. She was an elderly woman, very beautiful, with pale skin. Her silver hair was gathered in a long braid, and her blue eyes were so deep I could see myself reflected in them. She wore a wonderful nightgown made of blue velvet.

I went inside the house. We sat down in the living room. The fire was still lit, even though it was already spring, and the warmth was so delightful it summoned long naps.

Holding a hot cup of tea, she said: *"I'm happy you visited me, but you're a tough one, and I don't believe you came here without a particular reason."*

"You're not wrong! The garden, ma'am, it's abandoned. It's so delicate and helpless; please give me permission to take care of it!" I answered in one breath.

She let go of the cup of tea, and it shattered into pieces on the floor.

Mrs. Annette looked at me and started crying. I stood up immediately from the armchair, and I hugged her tight. I don't remember how long we stood like that. I caressed her face and went straight home.

Later that night, I thought about the encounter again; her tears had the taste of a sweet memory. I decided I would take some time before seeing her again; I didn't want to upset her. She would reach out to me, and I would wait until that moment.

A few days went by, and she called me. She would be waiting for me in her house that afternoon. It was a fresh and bright day; the sun was high in the sky. I rang the bell; I was happy to see her. There were a lot of pictures on the table, and I immediately understood she was ready to tell me her story and about the mysterious secret of the garden.

She was a young girl when she met the one that would have become her husband, her first and only love. The mansion was a gift from him, he built it brick by brick, and the garden was the most precious jewel it had. He was a perfect gardener, and he took care of the plants and their flowers as if they were his children. He often talked to them, and they repaid him by bearing fruits and wonderful flowers.

Annette's husband one day told her: "*In this garden, everything is beauty and love: my love for you.*"

Wind, rain, or hot weather could not prevent him from taking care of his garden. He worked there for hours on end, and before going back home, he always chose a different rose to take to his beloved Annette.

But one day, the cold north wind arrived and took away her beloved husband with an illness. Annette, grieving deeply, decided no one would have permission to touch the garden, and she put a fence around it.

Mrs. Annette closed her photo album, and while caressing my hands, she said: "*Now, my dear, run to the house and give new life to the garden. Give it new light, and make it shine again,*" she said, touched.

I hugged her; we didn't need any other words.

A lot of days of hard work and commitment were required, but then it finally looked like the garden was ready to talk to me. Every tree, plant, or bush seemed to start breathing again. Even the fountain came to life, and pure and fresh water finally gushed out from it. I cleaned my face with that water; I opened my arms and took a deep breath, filling my lungs. Everything was beautiful!

And while I write this story, Mrs. Annette is here, next to me, smiling in her beloved and unforgettable garden.

What does this story teach us?

Life is like a train journey. The trip has different stops, some delightful and some abrupt, but we must not stop, and we must not get off the train either. We must start again, believe in ourselves, and enjoy the trip. Until the very end.

My friend, Simon - Florence, Italy

The sun came through mischievously in my room. The air was changing, it was quite bracing, but I was so tired that I struggled to open my eyes. It was the last week of summer, and I wanted to enjoy it for a little while longer. So, I turned over to the other side of the bed, and I tried to fall asleep again.

With nothing else to do, that sly sun lit up my whole room.

"I understand; it's late. You're telling me I have to get up!"

I moved the sheets to the side of the bed, and I placed my feet on the floor. I opened my arms and yawned so loudly that Oliver, my furry dog, jumped from the armchair.

The house was quiet because everyone had started working again in my family, but for me, it was the last week of vacation before going back to school.

I have to admit I felt ready but a little dazed. It wasn't that easy to leave my old school behind: the friends, the teachers, and, most important of all, my trusted deskmate.

Well, yes, there were still a few days left before the middle school's bell would ring.

The new school bag, the books, the pencil case, the recently-bought jeans, and the clean and ironed t-shirt: they were all already on the armchair next to my desk.

I got this from my mom; I'm stubbornly precise and tidy. I hugged Oliver, and he was a mountain of fur. I went to the kitchen, and while I was dunking my chocolate chip cookie in a smoking cup of tea, Simon, my best friend, knocked at my door.

"Are you still in your pajamas? Come on, go and get changed immediately. I'll wait for you outside; you have five minutes!" he demanded.

"Ok, I'll be quick!" I answered. I believe I beat the record; before I knew it, I was ready!

Simon was my deskmate, my trusted friend. We've known each other since preschool; we spend a lot of time together. We're the opposite in every aspect, physically and temperamentally, but we get along. One is the strength of the other.

Simon is a small guy; I'm a beanpole. He's pot-bellied; I'm thin. He wears glasses that are so thick he can't see anything if he doesn't wear them; I don't. He has chestnut-colored hair and eyes with a funny mole on the right corner of his lip, while I have green eyes and black hair.

He's a little clumsy and funny, too; he makes me laugh a lot. He's my best friend, and the thought of not having him next to me in class makes me really sad, but I am curious to find out who my next deskmate will be.

Simon wasn't just like a friend to me; he was like a brother. I'm an only child and having him next to me every day made me feel less alone.

Oh, I'm such a scatterbrain; I haven't introduced myself yet!

I'm Lorenzo, and I'm eleven years old! I've started middle school, and it wasn't easy, but now I'm calm.

My story is a beautiful one: of friendship, bravery, strength, but most of all, of growth. Florence is my city, the cradle of Italian culture. Every culture, every street, and every alley remind us of times gone past when everything was made of beauty and talent. Every artist has their own mural; every bridge has its river, and every belltower has its church.

One afternoon at the end of summer, Simon and I, like every afternoon, went to play at the river.

Near our houses, there was a beautiful forest that hugged the riverbank. It wasn't very popular, and that's why Simon and I liked it. Our hair blowing in the wind, we would have bare feet and play in the water. What a laugh!

Suddenly, Simon came out of the water, and I saw his face was full of anger. I knew him well, and I immediately understood that something was upsetting him.

I came out of the water too, dripping, and I sat next to him under the big oak tree.

Simon started crying and put his arms around my neck.

I hadn't ever seen him cry - I liked Simon for this reason, too: he never moaned; he was always cheerful.

"Why are you so sad?" I asked thoughtfully.

"In a few days, we'll attend different schools, and you'll forget about me. You'll make new friends, and they're definitely going to be funnier," he answered, sobbing.

I smiled at him immediately. How silly! How could I forget about him?

A friend is a friend forever, especially if that friend is Simon.

I tried to comfort him and to make him laugh. I promised him I would never abandon him.

"My hands are soaking; if we don't hurry and dry off to put our clothes on, we'll turn into eels!" he said to me, laughing.

Summer afternoons with Simon were always fun. We never got bored, and there was always something fun to do. Boredom was unknown to us. So, after a wonderful summer, the first day of middle school arrived.

I was a little nervous, and the night before, I took Oliver to bed with me. Hugging him calmed me down; he loved being cuddled. I had breakfast early, and I went out of the house immediately; I had to meet Simon at 7:30 at the bus stop.

So, there he was, my dear friend. Seeing him made me feel instantly better.

He was wearing so many colors I couldn't understand his outfit, but I didn't say anything to him. Simon was quite touchy, and when he got into a mood, it was difficult to cheer him up.

We sat next to each other on the bus, and while recalling our funny summer adventures, we burst out laughing. After a few stops, a group of boys got on the bus. They were definitely our age but looked more cunning. I immediately thought that we were going to be in trouble.

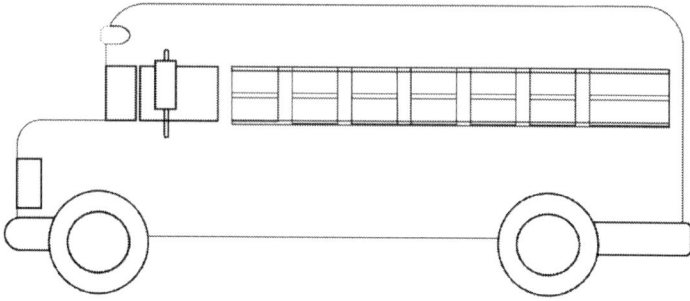

They were all dressed the same, but without personality, I might add: torn-up jeans, large t-shirts, backward hats, and an annoying and sticky chewing gum in their mouths. They arrived near our seats noisy, and the leader of the group gave a nudge to Simon and said: "*Move, butterball. What are you wearing? You look like a rainbow!*"

Simon looked at me; his eyes filled with tears, and without saying anything, he moved. Behind us, there was an annoying chattering.

Simon got off the bus not long after as he had arrived at the stop for his new school. We hugged and said we would meet each other in the afternoon.

"How can you be friends with a boy like that? He's a silly butterball!" one of the guys of that loud group said to me immediately.

"He's Simon, and he's my best friend. How strange. If you had a true friend, you wouldn't talk like that," I answered.

The boy didn't flinch, and while chewing his chewing gum nervously, he went back to his seat.

I finally got to school; that hour on the bus was truly unforgettable. I didn't like arguing, but I had to defend Simon.

I was excited, and without wasting time, I went into the classroom. It was still empty; they were all waiting for the bell to ring to go to class.

"Wow!" How beautiful the new school was! My classroom was very bright; the room overlooked a wonderful garden that was very cared for.

After a few minutes, the class was full, well, actually not totally full. Another ten minutes after the bell had rung, the classroom door opened wide. Such chaos! The teacher started yelling: *"What kind of confusion is this? Does it look like the appropriate time to get to class? We're getting off to a bad start!"*

When I saw the group of loud and rude boys, I put my hand to my face. Well, yes, it was them - the boys from the bus. I couldn't believe it!

They sat next to me, and from that moment on, listening to the teacher became a challenge.

When I got home, I told Simon everything, and I tried to find a solution to this mess.

Several months went by, and every day was the same. My classmates targeted Simon, and I saw him becoming more and more upset.

Simon was very odd, but he was my best friend, and he was perfect the way he was. He didn't have to change one bit.

One day, without any warning, the teacher decided to test everyone orally in the class; no one was excluded. I was calm because I had studied, but I saw the leader of the bus group become nervous. I hadn't ever seen him like that before: he was always a loudmouth, but I must admit that, even though he was lazy, he was very intelligent. If he put in some effort, he would get good results, for sure. I don't know what made me do it, but I moved closer.

"If you want, we can revise the chapters together. They're not very hard, and they're really interesting," I said, smiling.

All his friends laughed in my face, patting me on the back, but he didn't. He stood still, motionless, just looking at me.

He got up from his desk and said to me: *"I want to become a lawyer when I'm older, just like my grandfather."*

We were all speechless; there was complete silence in that room. Then he started again: "*I'm not a bully. I act like one, so I can be the center of attention.*"

I smiled when he said those words; I knew there was good in that boy. So, he sat next to me, I opened the book, and I explained everything to him in no time. His group of friends was amazed by his change of behavior, but he was their leader, so they listened without saying a word.

The oral test was amazing, he answered all the questions, and everyone was astonished. Everyone but me.

I talked for a long time with the boy with the ripped jeans, and I told him about the many, many, many times Simon made me laugh. He was impressed by my cheerfulness and promised me he would apologize. The next morning, like every morning, the rowdy group got on the bus. Simon was nervous.

The leader of the group moved closer like every morning, but this time he took off his hat, and he said: "*Lorenzo told me your name is Simon and you're his best friend! Nice to meet you, Simon; I'm Filippo, and I'm a friend of his too."*

Simon looked at me confused, and without blinking, he said: *"Do you know how to swim? You can come with us this afternoon! Oh, but I'm warning you: we can't come out of the river before our hands are wrinkly!"*

We all burst out laughing loudly, and we knew that the differences between us had gone.

It's been several years since that day, and Simon and I have another close friend. That's him, the boy with the ripped jeans, with his hat backward and the large t-shirt, but with a golden heart.

What does this story teach us?

Many people live in this beautiful land; we're all different and wonderfully imperfect.

Lorenzo, with his story, suggests just this. The friendship he has with his friend Simon, who is so different from him, makes him complete. Looking at the world with different eyes, we can notice all of its various shades: more beautiful horizons, bluer skies, faraway lands.

And that's how diversity becomes the winning strategy when presenting ourselves to the world.

ANTOINE AND CORINNE - PARIS, FRANCE

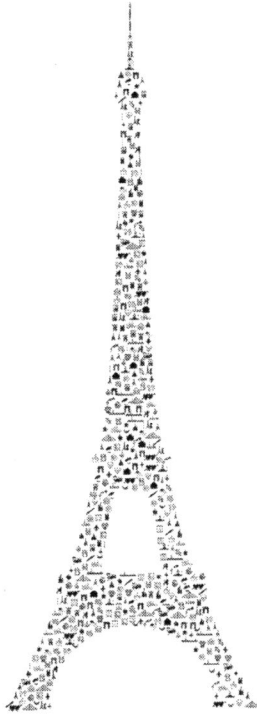

You could smell the perfume from the stairs of the big pink house. I thought it was a fragrant smell, a smell that no Parisian perfume shop could ever create.

I walked into her kitchen with white tiles, and I found her there, with her long hair, always in place, tied up in a bun.

She was never messy, and she smelled very good. When I hugged her, she smelled like caramel donuts, and her hands, always working, were soft and velvety.

A cake, freshly baked bread, or cookies with shapes so perfect it looked impossible they were handmade.

She moved around her kitchen with grace. Her steps were slow but always elegant. The warmth of the oven highlighted her cheeks like a spec of blush, and they became even redder. And when everything was perfect, ingredients and tools ready, she kneaded, mixed, sliced, and browned. Her hands turned into a magic wand: the only one that could make gourmet courses from a few simple ingredients.

She was a fairy!

And when one of her spells was in the oven, she would get her recipe book.

Every recipe was classified by moments about when the meal was best for; on what occasions, for example, only during the most special events. Everything was written in her unmistakable writing - it was elegant and round. Then, at the end of the recipe, she always left a thought, as if she wanted to print her love for cooking on that paper.

She's Corinne, and she's my grandmother!

I loved looking at her; it was impossible not to cuddle her tight.

I was really small when Mom left me at my grandma's during the afternoon. Fast as a rocket, I opened my books immediately, and I tried to hurry up and finish my homework as soon as possible so I could sit next to her on the stool in the kitchen.

I was her official helper; she called me Head Chef. With patience and expertise, she explained to me all the steps of every recipe. Every ingredient had a particular match, one of a kind. By looking at them on the counter by themselves, you couldn't tell they could turn in something so delicious.

Grandma was strict and meticulous in the kitchen. She said that technique was important, but what gave the final touch was passion alongside love.

I have to admit that when I tasted her dishes, I could feel her heartbeat, her hug's warmth; I felt her.

Every afternoon she told the story of that dish, where the ingredients came from, and the names of the tools she used. I listened, charmed and happy. I felt that what I was doing with my grandma came naturally to me. I didn't struggle, and I liked it a lot.

Grandma usually didn't give me any compliments. But, with a nod of her head, she let me know I had done a good job.

One afternoon at the end of October, you could hear the clinking of the raindrops on the windows of the big pink house and the rustling of the leaves, yellow at that point, of the big and old oak. The oven was still warm and, after doing a lot of work on the stove, Grandma took a tasty loaf of bread out of the oven - crunchy on the outside and soft on the inside.

She gave me a slice and said: *"When you make bread in your beautiful restaurant, remember to caress it before you slice it; that caress will get to me, up there."*

Many years went by, and Grandma was more and more tired, but she was always my favorite fairy.

She had left me her magic wand. I had become very good: technique and passion; these were Grandma's rules.

So, season after season passed, until fall arrived again, and with fall, the day of the choice was here.

Grandma was sitting in the blue velvet armchair, the wood crackling and burning in the big fireplace. She took my hand, brought it to her face, and she said: *"Antoine, the thing that makes you get up in the morning and just thinking about it makes you smile... that will be your choice."*

Grandma Corinne was very wise!

But maybe she was the only person who knew me more than anyone else.

I closed my eyes, softly caressed my grandma's soft face, and I answered: *"Grandma, I've already chosen!"*

My grandma smiled; she understood everything.

Paris was beautiful, very, very beautiful.

It was my city, the city I loved desperately - the most romantic city in the world.

Always a source of inspiration and attraction for artists and for lovers from all over the world. Every corner, bridge, and monument exudes beauty and is celebrated as if it was a woman loved to the point of madness.

It's the city of love and of curious, simple, and complicated people. It's a city that stays inside your heart.

Its bridges, the Seine, the bells of Notre-Dame, the blooming gardens, and the perfume of caramel in the alleys of the main road make it very special. Sometimes you can get the impression, by looking at it, that it is the artwork of an amazing painter.

While I was walking through the roads of the center, I thought: *"Could such a beautiful city ever be my adoptive mother?"*

I had sent out thousands of resumes across the whole of Paris, but no restaurant owner had replied. I didn't have any references; I didn't have a culinary background, and I hadn't ever worked in a professional kitchen.

Notre Dame's bells rang that morning in celebration. It was twelve o'clock on the first day of October, and while I was biting into an apple, sitting on the steps of the wonderful cathedral, my phone suddenly rang:

"*Is this Antoine?*"

"*Yes, this is he.*"

"*I need a busboy in my restaurant; I read your resume. If you want, you can have the job.*"

I felt my heart beating like crazy; it was clear I hadn't been called to work as an assistant chef. But I didn't lose heart; I had to start somewhere to make my dream come true.

I closed my eyes, and before giving my answer, I heard in my mind the sentence that my grandma often used to say: one step, then another, then one more. In the end, the door will open.

"*I'll accept, and if you want, I can get there immediately,*" I answered.

I believe the restaurateur was impressed by how happy I was, so he gave me an appointment on the same day at five o'clock in the afternoon. I ran home and retrieved an old apron Grandma had made for me. I decided that would be my good-luck charm.

I got to the restaurant on time, composed and smartly dressed.

The restaurant's sign shocked me - *"Chez Corinne"* was written on it. I thought it was fate. The place was positioned strategically in the center of Paris, with a breath-taking view, and before entering, I thought to myself: one step, then another, then one more. In the end, the door will open.

The restaurant was beautiful: elegant, polished, in perfect Parisian style.

Everything was enchanting: the red velvet armchairs close to each table, the white tablecloths with hand-embroidered lace glided perfectly to the ground on the shiny parquet, the porcelain dishes, the crystal glasses, all so perfectly clean they would shine like diamonds, the elegance of the silverware. The *mise en place* was impeccable; I was really charmed by all this beauty. I immediately understood that, in this restaurant, people worked with seriousness but with a lot of passion too. And while I was looking at all of this brilliance, all of a sudden, a hand patted my shoulder.

"Antoine, you're perfectly on time; I love punctuality. Follow me to the kitchen," the man with a deep and hoarse voice said to me.

We introduced ourselves to each other, and I was so euphoric as I walked into the kitchen. I started telling him about my whole life and everything I had learned from my grandma.

So I talked, talked, and talked, my words slipping and flowing like a river in flood, but then the big man interrupted me:

"Antoine, this is a kitchen! Not a ladies hair salon!"

He was the chef, the head chef of that restaurant.

How exciting! His white uniform, perfectly pressed, glided down his lean body.

Tufts of his curly hair poked out from under the *toque blanche*: the hat that only a chef wears.

"Wow! What a shiny kitchen and clean chef - just like Grandma!" I exclaimed.

He immediately gave me the apron, and without any gestures, he showed me my place. I instantly realized that I had to work hard.

"The restaurant is always full, and the clients are very demanding, even when it comes to cleaning" the chef said.

"Chef, don't worry. I'm used to strictness; Grandma was always like a commander to me!" I answered.

The chef gave me a shy smile and made me sign the contract straight away.

I had done it; I was in a professional kitchen, like a real chef!

Not too long after, the rest of his staff team arrived.

As soon as they saw me, I felt like a gazelle in a pack of lions.

"I'm Antoine; I'm officially your busboy. From now on, dirt won't live long."

All of them doubled over with laughter.

I had just broken the ice a little bit when I heard the head chef yell: *"Guys, get into your positions. In less than an hour, the restaurant will be full."*

So, everyone went to their place. We looked like an assembly line. Everyone had a particular task and role in the kitchen, from slicing the vegetables to making the sauces, kneading, roasting, boiling, and wrapping.

Nothing was left to chance. Time flew by, and the place was as full as it could be within a few minutes. You could hear the client's steps walking into the restaurant, smell the perfumes of the elegant ladies, and listen to the sound of continuous talking and laughing.

I was very excited. And you might wonder: *"But, why, Antoine? You're only a busboy!"*

Yes, that's what I was, but I knew it was only the first step towards the goal.

The kitchen turned into an orchestra with the head chef as the conductor. He had perfect control over everyone, and they all listened to him. Well, actually, not all of them.

There was one person, the assistant chef, who worked alongside the head chef. He was his shadow. But, unlike the rest of the team, he was a know-it-all and unpleasant. He always had something to say, and nothing was good enough for him.

The chef ignored his tantrums; he was his prized stallion, and he couldn't replace him. He was so good!

While everyone else was cooking refined dishes, I was there, in my corner, with my hands in boiling water full of suds, washing towers of dishes and crockery.

But I couldn't miss out on the chance of learning. So, out of the corner of my eye, I watched them every minute. And every day, I learned the basics, secrets, highly sought-after recipes, and tricks a real chef should know.

My hands were so red by the end of the evening they looked like tomatoes; my legs were like planks of wood because of the exhaustion, but I wasn't discouraged, and I ran home. I dashed to the kitchen at night, and I remade the dishes the chef suggested. I had it all in my head; the steps, ingredients, and tools to use.

My secret?

The final touch.

There wasn't room for distraction and pauses in the kitchen. Everything had its incessant rhythm. One night, when the whole restaurant was full, a storm let loose in the kitchen:

"I'm tired of listening to you, following your lead, I want to stand out, and I quit!" the assistant chef said, throwing his apron on the counter as a challenge.

The chef didn't pick it up.

The kitchen froze, everybody stopped but me. I kept washing some beautiful crystal glasses without pausing.

"Antoine, leave the bubbles behind. Come here and work with me!" the head chef shouted.

I remembered everything, all the steps of every single recipe; I recognized the spices in every container by the smells. So, we started working, side to side, tirelessly, without pause, without speaking. We were in perfect harmony.

More than a year went by, and I kept working hard without ever complaining.

One night, it was dead of night; the whole team had just left. The head chef came closer and said: *"I'm tired. Do you want to steer this ship? Are you ready to be captain?"*

I brought a hand to my face immediately. I was so excited my brain turned to mush, and in a whisper, I answered: *"Yes, Chef, I'm ready."*

It's been more than ten years since that yes, and I'm still the captain of this beautiful ship. I have crossed several seas, at rest and in the storm, but I've never sunk.

I've created magic in the kitchen many times, mixing water, flour, and baking powder to create the tastiest and most fragrant thing I've ever eaten: bread.

And every time, before slicing it, I caress it. I close my eyes, and I find myself there, in the kitchen with the white tiles in Grandma's big pink house.

And she's there, with her long hair gathered in a chignon, smiling at me and saying: one step, then another, then one more. In the end, the door will open.

Where there's a will, there's a way. That's what reading this story inspires and suggests.

Antoine is a boy, just like you, he has his suitcase in his hand, the suitcase of his dreams.

Each of us has one. Sometimes we struggle to open it; sometimes, we even find it difficult to fill it. Dreams are desires, particular wishes that our hearts tell us.

They can become real only if we want them to. That powerful strength that every one of us has only needs to be fed with determination, grit, and courage. Everything is possible; nothing is impossible.

And, if sometimes the dream seems unreachable, we should believe in it even more. Let's look up to the sky; there's always a star that will light the way.

SHINING LIGHTS - NEW YORK, AMERICA

I always waited anxiously for nightfall. After a long and exhausting day in the office, taking off my shoes in the doorway to my home, putting on comfortable clothes, and sipping an americano relaxed me and calmed me down. I had the feeling my heartbeat would take on a slower rhythm, less accelerated and my mind was finally free from the thoughts.

I lived in a small apartment in Harlem, New York, in the most colorful block in the city. They had recommended other apartments to me in trendier blocks, but when I saw this one, I knew that it had to be mine.

Harlem is a neighborhood where you can immediately breathe in life. There have always been a lot of people of all races and colors, and, listening to the music that came out of the pubs, you could hear every single instrument. That smell, embracing and intrusive, of spices in every corner, made me feel like a citizen of the world.

My ungenerous alarm clock always rang very early. The city lights were still lit, and a foggy air in the sky gave the impression of being in a timeless place.

I always wore a heavy coat, wrapped a long and soft scarf around my neck, and went to the subway. I was always in a hurry, I always made the same trip, and I never noticed the people near me.

Since I moved to New York, I have become reluctant to engage with the worldliness of the city, and I lived quite a withdrawn life. This may be because when you live in such a big city, you always put off the good occasions to go out as you think there's time always to live them in the future.

As soon as I got to New York, my first goal was to find a job. So one day, many years ago, sitting on the subway and reading a newspaper, I saw an advertisement for a publishing house that was looking for a secretary. I thought to myself; I'll try. The worst thing that could happen would be for them to say no.

Instead, they hired me straight away - without giving me the chance to organize myself! The day after the interview, I was already sitting at that desk. I had my hair combed into a perfect '60s hairstyle, and there was a pale-yellow phone that rang constantly.

The publishing house was very famous in New York. It belonged to a rich and extravagant Italian editor who arrived in America on a cruise ship. He was only supposed to stay for two weeks, but he fell in love with the city and decided to stay permanently.

New York was, in fact, a city where dreams really could become true.

It's so majestic and beautiful that you can forgive it for everything: the never-ending noise, the traffic, how big it is, the distance between places. It's the city of skyscrapers, big shop windows, musicals, majestic theaters, businessmen with overnight cases, and everything is possible, here and now.

I, too, had been enticed by the shining lights, and even though I knew full well that I was going to be wasted as a secretary in that office, I accepted immediately.

Ever since I was a little kid, I have dreamed of becoming a writer. My grandma saved all my stories and always told me that, one day, when I became famous, my first autograph would be for her.

I loved writing, but I had low self-esteem. Every time I wrote something, I tore up the paper or screwed it into a ball and threw it away. Then I tried again, but my stories were always imperfect to me. I immediately gave up and packed away my pen and paper.

But if Mohammed won't come to the mountain, the mountain will come to Mohammed. And that's how it happened.

In the office, I was always busy making appointments, checking the planner, and organizing other people's days. It was only during my lunch break that I could devote my time to my favorite hobby: writing.

The boredom of that office made me find my magic flow, and I was like a waterfall. I wrote, wrote, and wrote; words bloomed from my pen like scented flowers.

I wrote spontaneously, and I talked about my new American life, my habits, and those of the everyday people I had met in this wonderful city. I described my eccentric office boss, a rich man, a little bit crazy, who always wore a full evening suit, had a pipe in his mouth, and Jack Daniel's on the rocks on his desk. Then my neighbor on the same floor as me, a slightly-hostile woman with ruffled hair who left the house wearing her pink silk robe and said it was *chic*. I wrote about a very elegant Chinese woman who always sat in the same spot on the subway. She had a broach on her coat, and she gracefully enjoyed a chocolate chip cookie while wearing black lace gloves. I also featured a group of young boys who sped past my office each day on their skateboards, at the same time and with the same enthusiasm. I wrote on loose white sheets of paper, and I was never organized; I left them everywhere on my desk. No one would care about me being messy. I was alone in my room, and no one, not even by mistake, could get in there.

One day I left my room. I don't know what I had in my head that morning, but I was so fuzzy-headed that I didn't see my office boss. Belly against belly, we crashed into each other, and all the papers of my stories flew like airplanes all over the corridor. What a disaster!

My face was red, and my heart was pounding like a drum. I kneeled on the floor, and, crawling like a snail, I tried to gather up all the sheets of paper.

But a huge hand stopped me and took away all my material.

Oh, no, I could already see *"the end"* written on my desk.

"*Sophia, is this what you do all day? Scribbles, just useless scribbles, I imagine. Now get back to your phone,*" the office boss said.

I felt so humiliated that later that night, when I got home, I thought it was going to be my last day at work. And while I was sipping my usual americano, the phone rang.

"*Hi Sophia, am I interrupting you? Would you like to come by the office? I must talk to you!*"

I anxiously put the phone down. What a mess, it was my boss, and he was probably angry because of the story about him.

"*Silly, how silly, how incredibly silly,*" I repeated to myself.

I put on my coat, tied my scarf around my neck, and went to the office. He was there, wearing his usual evening suit, pipe in his mouth and Jack Daniel's on the rocks on his desk. I was so scared that my legs were shaking like crazy.

He let me sit down.

"Sophia, are you the author of those stories?"

Oh, gosh! I could have said a big and enormous NO, but I'm an awful liar, and if I had lied, my boss would have known the exact opposite.

"Yes, that's me," I answered in a whisper.

He stood up from his armchair like a rocket; he came towards me and grabbed me firmly by the shoulders. *"My girl, you're a talent. You made me laugh, think, and I was so moved by your stories, I hoped you were the one who wrote them."*

I don't know how long we sat in his room talking and planning big things.

It's been several years since that crazy night.

I'm still here, in my colorful and musical apartment in Harlem; my alarm still wakes me up early, and the road I take is always the same one to my old office. I don't have a '60s hairstyle, and I don't answer the pale-yellow phone anymore. I write stories, and I move people; I make them laugh and think with my tales.

I'm an author too, and I'm my own boss.

I hadn't ever thought I would feel so amazing and have the perfect balance between mind and heart one day.

What does this story teach us?

Believing in ourselves, in our abilities, not giving up, and trying and trying again is important.

Maybe we won't reach our goal every time, or perhaps we will realize that's not the right path for us, but at least we have lived, tried, and measured ourselves. We became better.

So let's go to the mirror, move our hair to one side, and let's wink at ourselves because we're perfect like this, perfect the way we are!

The Old Violin – Vlorë, Albany

It's where the waters of the Adriatic Sea meet the crystalline Ionian Sea, slipping from a straight and flat stretch with jagged rocks and sharp corners, that the bell tower of the small church in the city of Vlorë, a little outdated, still rang the tolls.

It was already noon and Nora, all out of breath, started packing.

They were two huge suitcases; she didn't have enough time to

prepare them, so she opened the wardrobe and put everything

inside: sweaters, scarves, hats, costumes, all in bulk, and

without a precise order, as she was used to doing.

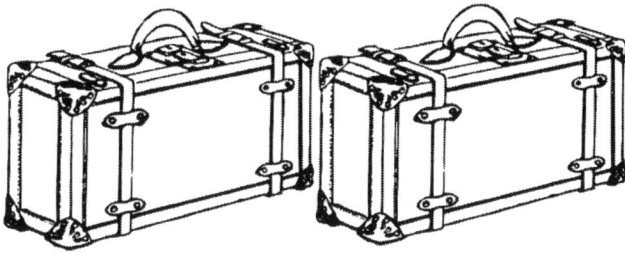

Inside her big house, right in the city center, practically only the

walls remained. It was so empty you could hear an echo. In the

previous days, Nora had got rid of most of her furniture; she had

sold it for a good price. She kept all her profits in a leather wallet

that she had bought with her first earnings. She promised herself

she would never ask for help from anyone.

The suitcases were on the bed and, on the only soft, blue sofa,

there was her violin.

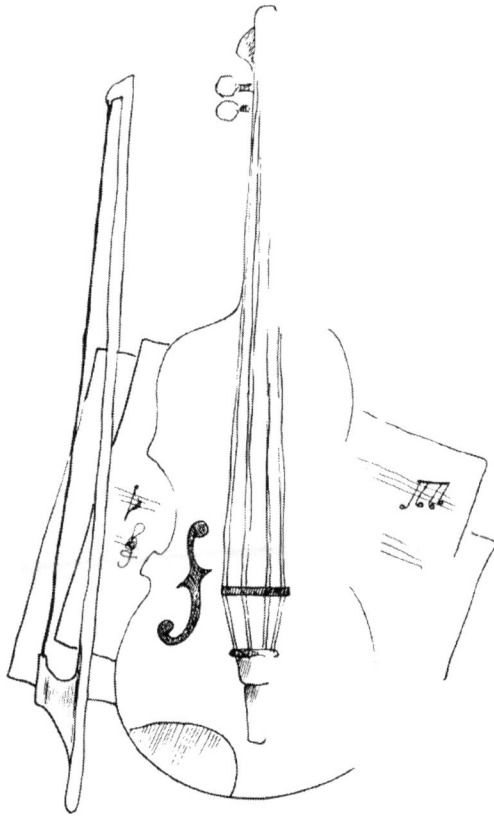

It was the oldest one in the city. She had bought it in a shop of an old carpenter; it was made purely with wood from a cherry tree. It was the most precious thing she owned. Oh no, let me correct myself; the most precious thing was her daughter, Meghi.

Several years previously, Nora had done brilliantly during her musical training at the conservatory, so once she completed her studies, she thought her life would change. She would finally realize her dream: teaching. She had read that there was already an open spot for a teacher at the conservatory.

She waited, sitting composedly on the armchair of her house, for long and endless days until the phone rang.

"Nora Sula?"

"Yes, it's me," Nora answered.

"You're in. There's an open spot; you've got the job!"

"Yeeees!" She was so happy she hung up the phone without saying thank you.

And she danced, danced, and danced around the whole house until she fell down on the cold floor, tired but happy. She called her boyfriend immediately, and just like she always dreamt, he arrived with a bouquet of yellow tulips, her favorite flowers, playing the heart's waltz. That's how the two sealed a promise; a week later, they got married. The celebration lasted for three days; there were a lot of relatives, and they had to make them happy.

During the spring of the following year, a delicate cry woke up the whole block. It was little Meghi. Finally, she was born; chubby and with a full head of blonde hair. Her grandma, on hearing about her birth, hung a pink bow on the big front door.

Meghi grew up surrounded by infinite love from her family, but suddenly, everything changed.

"Why aren't you at home? Our daughter needs you too," Nora said to her husband.

"Why can't you understand, Nora? This is an opportunity I can't miss. Vienna is waiting for me; that's where I have to go."

And he left, violently slamming the door behind him.

Nora's husband was a great cellist, and he was called up by Vienna's orchestra to play in concerts with them for a year.

Nora immediately felt alone, but in her arms, Meghi was smiling. *"We're not alone, Mom. There's your music with us,"* Meghi answered, delicately caressing her mom.

Nora didn't lose heart, and she went straight to the living room. Meghi went to her bedroom to choose a beautiful dress to wear. She returned to her mom and sat down to listen.

Nora's hands skipped daintily up and down her violin's strings. The music and the notes echoed around the whole house. Nora and Meghi laughed so much, then they came together in a long, tight hug, like the ones they liked.

It had been exactly one year since Meghi's father went away. No phone calls, no contact; it seemed like he was gone forever. For this reason, Nora had decided to sell the family home and make some new memories with Meghi.

The very day that they were scheduled to move, the postman knocked on the door.

Nora's heart immediately started beating faster. The woman ripped a huge yellow letter from his hands and closed the door. She sat on the sofa, her legs were trembling, and her hands couldn't hold the letter still. And she read it, read it and read it again and again.

It ended like this: *"I'm mortified, but I have realized I can't be a father; I need to be alone. I loved you, but now you need to think about you and your baby girl."*

These words echoed in her head like the tolls of the bell tower that had just rung at noon. She had no tears.

Nora closed the letter, opened Meghi's bedroom door, and she said: *"What do you say? Are you ready to go to Italy?"*

Meghi smiled at her, she was a very smart kid, and maybe she understood it all. *"Of course! Are the suitcases ready, Mom?"* So, without wasting any more time, and without thinking about it any further, Nora took the suitcases and closed the house's door behind them.

The old bus was about to leave, and Nora and Meghi arrived at the bus stop out of breath. Nora put their suitcases on the bus, and before the doors closed, she took a final look at the bell tower of the church in ruins and smiled. She knew she was doing the right thing.

So, Nora and Meghi left Albany forever.

The trip was tiring, the bus' air was stale, but Nora and Meghi were too happy to complain.

"Mom, do we know someone in Brindisi?" the child asked.

"Yes, love, there's an old man waiting for us."

"An old man, Mom? Can I call him grandpa?"

Nora smiled and said: *"Of course, my love!"*

Through a friend she had in Rome, Nora had the phone number of an old man who needed assistance in his wonderful mansion near the seaside. In Brindisi.

So they arrived and stood still, motionless like statues in front of the steel gate to the mansion close to the beach.

The daughter of the old man opened the gate, welcomed them with a bright smile, and said: *"Nora, is that you? What a pleasure! We've been waiting for you!"*

Nora knew Italian as television in Albany aired a lot of Italian programs, and she thought it was a musical language.

She looked at the woman, nodded, and she slid her hand slide down Meghi's long hair, which was tied back with a long pink silk ribbon.

It was the child who answered the lady: *"Of course, it's my mom!"* Meghi spoke Italian well too. She was an intelligent child, always curious.

The old man was sitting on a big green velvet armchair, next to the fireplace in the big living room. The room was bright; the sun came powerfully through the big glass window overlooking the sea. The old man smoked a pipe, and the smoke that came out of it looked like it was doing somersaults.

Meghi placed the suitcase on the floor and said: *"I'm Meghi. Do you want to be my grandpa?"*

The old man burst out laughing so loud and hard that he dropped his pipe. While he was picking it up with his wrinkly and knobby hand, he said: *"Calm down, baby girl, don't be in a hurry!"*

Nora was happy and proud of her child. But even though she had a roof and a hot meal every day, she missed her violin made of cherry tree wood.

It had been resting for too long in its red velvet case.

"Don't worry, Nora, you'll see that a school will call you soon. You've sent more than a thousand resumes around, don't worry," the old man said, patting her on the shoulder.

And just when her hopes were about to disappear, the phone rang: *"Nora Sula? A place has become vacant in an old music school in town; do you accept?"* a raspy voice said.

"*Yeees!*" Nora answered.

How strange; they were almost the same words she had heard many years ago in her city. She hung up the phone, hugged the old man, and held him tight. And she danced, danced and danced, like last time, before falling down, exhausted but happy.

The following day, she woke up early. She had carefully ironed her white silk shirt the night before. She pinned a silver broach to her chest as it was her grandma's good luck charm. She applied a touch of make-up and went to the school.

Many long years went by, and Nora was sipping a cup of tea sitting on the sofa in the huge living room.

A ray of sunshine shone through the glass window, and Meghi suddenly asked: "*Mom, we're happy, aren't we?*"

Nora smiled delicately and answered: "*Yes, we're happy, we always have been.*"

So Nora and Meghi hugged each other tight, just how they liked it.

What does this story teach us?

We think about our life as a road - a long path that we must travel.

The path can scare you sometimes because the road in front of us isn't always straight. We can come across a tight curve, a difficult climb, unpaved streets. Staying still isn't the solution. We always have to keep moving.

This story can make us think a lot. Nora packs her bags; she leaves everything she knows, her comfort, to start a new path. Strength and courage become faithful squires that make her proud and brave, ready to take her life into her hands and make it beautiful.

We're the ones who lead our destiny; we're the ones who decide how to drive, who to go along with. We're the ones who have to start the car and go.

The path may look long and torturous but, in the end, we always come home.

EPILOGUE

What do I have that makes me special?

This is the question that all the main characters in these seven stories ask themselves.

All of them have a fire inside - the fire of curiosity, grit, and determination. The water that puts out their insecurities and inadequacies that act like a thin string that leaves us hanging.

Every story has a happy ending because the characters truly want it. Their strength breaks down the barriers: the ones of fear, uncertainty, and fragility.

All characters find themselves in front of the mirror just as they are: in their simplicity, uniqueness, honesty. By looking at themselves, they understand that's their winning weapon, the only key that opens their door.

When I wrote these stories, I imagined the characters in their entirety: physically, temperamentally, even down to their smallest features, and I felt like I was drawing their profile.

I found all of them to be wonderfully perfect. Unique. Unique just the way they were. Unique like you: different from the others, but true, very true to yourself.

I hope from the bottom of my heart that this book, these stories, might leave an impression in your heart and mind. I have put down a small pebble to mark your way.

I hope that every time you feel the need, every time you feel a little down, far away from yourself, you might pick it up and read it again. To find yourself again, to feel simply and wonderfully perfect. Perfect the way you are.

So you'll finally feel at home.

Made in the USA
Las Vegas, NV
20 December 2024